# Raising Ryan

# Raising Ryan

Written and Compiled By
Corinne Derenburger

Copyright © 2004 by Corine Derenburger

ISBN 0-7414-1783-9

*Published by:*
**INFINITY**
PUBLISHING.COM
*519 West Lancaster Avenue*
*Haverford, PA 19041-1413*
*Info@buybooksontheweb.com*
*www.buybooksontheweb.com*
*Toll-free (877) BUY BOOK*
*Local Phone (610) 520-2500*
*Fax (610) 519-0261*

*Printed in the United States of America*

*Printed on Recycled Paper*

*Published November 2003*

# Table of Contents

## Dedication

To Ryan, you are my teacher. You have taught me what is really important in life. You have given me unconditional love and you've taught me *how* to give unconditional love. You are my example of how to trust God by you trusting me. You've taught me about not taking things for granted. You have taught me to forget my own needs, desires, and dreams. You've taught me how to give unselfishly not expecting anything in return. Most of all, you've taught me how to hope and to have faith. You have taught me the biggest and most valuable life lessons I've ever learned. When I grow up, I want to be like you.

## Preface

Dear Reader,

As Elisa Morgan and Carol Kuykendall from MOPS®
International would say, when a child is born, a
mother is born as well. I agree. In my case of
becoming a mother for the fourth time, I became a
mother of a special needs child. So 'when a child
with special needs is born, a mother with special
needs is born as well.'

You might be asking yourself, "What is MOPS?" MOPS
stands for Mothers of Preschoolers. MOPS
International based in Denver, Colorado is a non
profit, non denominational organization. Their
purpose is to nurture *every* mother of preschooler by
meeting her distinct needs to the glory of Jesus
Christ. At this time there are over 3,000 groups that
meet world-wide. Ryan was only one-year old when I
found this wonderful group of MOPS moms at my
local church. The friends I made through this ministry
continue to support me as I fumble my way through
*Raising Ryan*.

My hope and prayer for you is that you gain insight,
hope, and encouragement by reading through this
book, *Raising Ryan*.

## Special Thanks

To my Lord and Savior, the Lover of my soul, Jesus Christ for giving me the gift of writing and for allowing me the humble privilege of raising Ryan

To Denise Bennett Horn for using your editing talents on this book and for giving me honest advice ☺

To my husband, Todd, for pushing me through this work and keeping me focused on my calling and purpose

To my eldest son and daughters, Matt, Sarah, Jessica, and Hannah for being loving siblings to Ryan

To my Pastor and his wife, Fred and Valerie Bennett for blessing me and urging me to pursue writing

To Pastor Chris and Becky Bennett for praying for me every step of the way

*In memory of Andrew Wells*

*July 4, 1996 to May 26, 2003*

## Introduction

Ryan is affectionately known as Boo-Boy or Ry-man for short. I don't know exactly how he earned his nick names, but they stuck.

In the beginning of this long journey, Ryan was born with the umbilical cord wrapped around his neck. We moved to Memphis, during the ice-storm of 1994, and I went into labor within the first twelve hours of being here. We drove around Interstate 240 and found Methodist South Hospital. The only people present during his birth were a nurse, my husband, and Jessica who was two. She was watching the Flintstones on TV, while I was giving birth. I had one contraction and Ryan came out with the umbilical cord wrapped around his neck and the nurse panicked. She started raising her voice at me telling me to push and push now! And I looked at Todd and said I don't have a contraction now. She loudly said, "I don't care, you have to push the baby out now!" So I took a deep breath and out he came. He was blue. Todd had a funny look on his face, but it wasn't the usual normal funny look he had on his face. The nurse whisked him away and I didn't see him for several hours. I kept calling the nursery over a period of about twelve hours and asking about Ryan and when he was coming to room in with me. I was told that he was blue and his body temperature was lower than normal. Ryan's body needed to adjust to normal temperature before I could see him. After about twelve hours, a nurse came in to clean me up and a doctor, who the hospital assigned me to, came in to check on me. Then finally, about dinner time, I saw Ryan for the first time. Neither my husband nor I knew what an incredible, enduring, exciting journey on which we were about to embark with our new little bundle of joy. At one point we sought to find out if there was any medical malpractice involved in Ryan's medical condition because there wasn't a doctor present. There were discrepancies in my medical records but because I delivered within forty-five minutes of arriving to the hospital, they are in the clear.

1

Looking back, I find it odd that I had prayed that this child would be content and happy. With my other four children, who are incidentally typical, I prayed for health. And indeed he is content. He is the most smiley *little* boy (he weighs over ninety pounds) I've ever seen. Even though he is handicapped and doesn't communicate through words, he laughs and squeals with joy eighty-five percent of the time. He gives unconditional love and kisses by sitting on people's laps and leaning toward them as if he's giving us permission to kiss him. It's like he's saying in his own way, "You may have the honor and privilege of kissing my adorable face."

I've discovered that being a mother and especially of a special needs child means having good days and better days. Some days are filled with wonder and amazement as Ryan shows signs of progression and accomplishment. Others contain thoughts of hopelessness and regression. Walking by faith is a moment by moment journey with God. Knowing that God loves Ryan more than I love Ryan is essential to not walking by what I see. I try and look at Ryan through God's eyes and think of how hard it must be for Him to restrain from completely healing Ryan. There must be a greater glory that will come about from Ryan being in the physical and mental state he is in than I can imagine.

## Being Thankful is a State of Mind

Ryan has taught me to be thankful for the simple things in life. All the basics of life I took for granted with the other children, I can't with him. Ryan's accomplishments of crawling and walking didn't come easily. At nine years old, he's still working on playing with toys, running, potty training, self dressing, and interacting with others. He is my human example of love. He loves me unconditionally. He loves me the way I'm to love others. When he does something kind he does so with no strings attached. All he requires is time; time cleaning him, time holding him, time dressing him, time praying over him, time loving on him. He is the perfect picture of how I am supposed to be with God. Ryan is one hundred percent dependant on my taking care of him. I speak for him, clothe him, clean up after him, clean him up after he gets himself into a mess, protect him, and provide for him. Time is the only investment in which I can't get a return. I can invest money, but I can always make more money. I can't make more time. When it's gone, it's gone.

## Sometimes *It* Happens

Ryan leaves his mark where ever he goes. Sometimes I have thought of him like an artist. As a friend of mine says, "Ryan's poop is his medium and the world is his canvas." Many days I go through the "sanitizing the house" mode. This is when Ryan feels that he needs to dust the furniture and everything else with the contents of his stinky diapers. He also likes to let *it* go in the bathtub as well. I'll be giving him a bath when he starts giggling hysterically and flapping his arms as if he was a chicken trying to fly. Undoubtedly he has pooped in the tub and he is hurling it all over the bathroom. *'It'* lands on walls, mirrors, the floor, the wallpaper, and you guessed it, me. It's a good thing I wear glasses because they act as shields for my eyes. It's quite a scene, and I get asked all the time how I deal with that, especially on a daily basis. And my answer is, "I just do." This brings truth to the scripture '...by the grace of God go I.'

## Sometimes *It* Doesn't

I've learned that nothing is too small to be thankful for. I find myself thankful when Ryan throws dirt all over the front porch because it's not poop. I find myself thankful when Ryan grabs a handful of yogurt and flings it all over me because it's not poop. I'm thankful that when he gives me a bear hug and I have blood all over my clothes from his massive bloody nose because it's not poop. I rejoice when he throws hotdogs at me because it's not poop. When he plasters it all over the front porch, all I have to do is hose it down. I've considered investing in a rubber house, vinyl furniture, a sprinkler system, with an installed alarm system. That way when he gets poop everywhere, all I have to do is sound the alarm and everyone evacuates the house while the sprinklers come on and spray off all the furniture, walls, fixtures, and gives him a shower as well. And when he does poop inside the potty, I'm elated!

## Thank God for the Small Stuff

One time I was putting Ryan's socks and shoes on him, when I picked up the right shoe and he was holding his left · leg up in the air and he saw what shoe I had and switched legs. Moments like these bring me tears of gladness. One night, he was eating a banana and he actually held it for more than two bites with out squishing it between his fingers. Another time he pushed me down onto the sofa and climbed up into my lap. He pressed his face into mine and held it to kiss me. Well, he slobbered on me but I knew what he meant to do. One day my oldest daughter was typing on the computer and Ryan brought her a block of cheese from the refrigerator for her to open. He actually threw the cheese at her, but nevertheless, he brought it to someone to open for him. The first time he fed himself was when he was almost three. He picked up a pickle from his Dad's plate and sucked on it. One time he actually signed please and thank you.

## Wouldn't It Be Nice?

Wouldn't it be nice if you could comprehend like other boys do,
And you could play with your toys the way you were meant too?
Wouldn't it be nice if you could run and play sports?
And you could dress yourself in tennis shoes, tank tops and shorts?
Wouldn't it be nice if you were potty trained and self assured?
And you could wear 'big boy pants' and not look like a nerd?
Wouldn't it be nice if you could communicate with words?
And not have you so frustrated when I misread your utters,
Wouldn't it be nice if you could tell me what's wrong,
And we wouldn't play a guessing game that's 2 hours long?
Wouldn't it be nice if you could comb your own hair with a comb?
And you could brush your own teeth, and answer the phone?
Wouldn't it be nice if you could fix your own snacks after school?
And feed yourself with utensils and sit on your own bar stool?
Wouldn't it be nice if you could bathe by yourself and take your own showers?
And we could spend time the way others do during their waking hours?
Wouldn't it be nice if you could tease your sisters like brothers do?
And have friends to spend the night with, and buddies who visited you?
Wouldn't it be nice if we could understand things the way you do and see?
And that I could teach you just as much as you've taught me?
Like how to be content and thankful for the little things in life,
Like walking, shopping at the mall, or even riding a bike.
And wouldn't it be nice if I could just hear aloud one time,

'Hi Mommy, my name is Ryan and I will love you for all of my life'
And wouldn't it be nice if I didn't compare you to another,
And I would realize and accept the fact that *I am* the world's most blessed mother.

## Bone Crusher

One day when Ryan was about eighteen months old, it was my favorite time of the day, naptime! I picked up both Hannah, Ryan's younger sister, at the time age six months, and Ryan. I went to put Hannah down first for her nap and I adjusted Ryan over my shoulder like a sack of potatoes. I laid Hannah in her crib and came out to shut the door. Well, the door stuck and wouldn't close all the way. I checked the floor by the entry way of Hannah's room and nothing, so I tried closing it again. Finally, it's shut. WHAAA! I heard Ryan scream the most blood curdling scream I've ever heard. This was the first time, Ryan cried. He even had tears. He was flailing around and grabbed my glasses off my face and chucked them somewhere. With me not being able to see a thing, I saw red everywhere. I quickly opened Hannah's door and then I saw it. There was blood everywhere; all over me, the carpet, the hallway, Hannah's door, and Ryan. I dropped to the floor with Ryan in my arms. I held Ryan up close to me checking him. I had closed his finger in Hannah's door and it was hanging by his fingernail. I was sickened. Not by the bloody mess, but the fact that I had crushed my baby's finger. I called my neighbor to tell her what happened and she rushed right over because she couldn't hear me over the top of Ryan's screaming. She walked right on in and asked me where my glasses were. I told her that Ryan had grabbed them and flung them somewhere. After what seemed like hours of looking, she found my glasses behind the hall bathroom door. I put on my 'eyes' and I finally saw everything that happened. Poor Ryan! We rushed him to the doctor's office and as soon as we arrived, they escorted us immediately to a room. I'd never had such fast service at a physician's office before! Once the doctor came in to see Ryan, she and a couple of nurses papoosed him onto a gurney so they could work on him. This immediately calmed him down and he went to sleep. They sewed his finger back on and we went home to clean up the mess. By the time Ryan's Dad, got home, Ryan was fine. I was called Bone Crusher for about a year after that incident.

## Firsts We Take For Granted

First step, first word, first smile, first rolling over, first laugh, first self-feeding, first bottle, first drink out of a spill proof cup, first drink out of a big kid cup, first restaurant outing, first pre-school, first grocery store shopping experience, first friend, first friend to sleep over, first extra-curricular activity, first day of school, first bike, first Christmas etc. All these things we assume as parents will occur with our children during the time frame the books or charts tell us that they will happen. But what if they don't? What if the firsts you so badly desired don't come during that expected time or worse, what if they don't ever come to pass? That's when you decide to become thankful for the little and simple things in life.

# Ryan's Firsts

Ryan didn't roll over until he was well over the age of two. He even had a bald spot on the back of his head because he just laid there. Where ever I would lay him, there he'd stay. Which I have to admit it was nice being able to always find him when I came back looking for him. Shortly after he was two, he could sit up propped up with pillows. For about a year, Ryan just sat there. Then when he was three years old, he began to crawl. But before that he just pulled himself around on the floor dragging his lower body around. He became mobile when he was about thirty months old. It was about that time we got him an adaptive device called a K-Walker. Ryan didn't take his first step until he was almost three and that was with the K-walker. A K-Walker is a backwards walking device meant to aid the patient in walking as steadily as he or she can. It has four wheels and almost wraps around the patient's body. Some K-Walkers even have a seat so when the child gets tired they can sit for awhile. Ryan would try and walk without it but usually ended up falling because he kept letting go. He was walking by faith. He must've been picturing himself walking in his mind. And every time he would come out of his walker he'd fall. He used his K-walker for about a year. One of his teachers the previous school year told me that Ryan would be walking by Thanksgiving. He would be three and a half by Thanksgiving. I pondered what she had told me for almost a year. His teacher told me that she prayed consistently for Ryan's health and ability. I thought, "Ok, cool." And as God would have it, Ryan walked on Thanksgiving Day at his aunt's house. He came out of the walker for the last and final time and didn't fall. I couldn't wait to come back and tell Ryan's teacher. Now that's truly something to be thankful for!

## Ryan's first word

I'm still waiting on that one! Although, his Dad believes that Ryan says Daddy all the time.

## Ryan's first smile and laugh

He came out of the womb smiling and laughing! He must know something we don't.

Ryan took a bottle for many years before he used a spill proof cup. He still drinks from a spill proof cup, as long as he can suck juice out of it, he's happy.

I'm still waiting for him to have a first friend who is a peer and his first sleep over party. That might have to take place up in Jesus' bedroom. I'm still waiting on the bike riding as well. I'd be thankful if he could just run steadily. One day though, he'll be riding a bike and running and jumping like all the other boys do.

## Ryan's first day of school

Ryan has been in school since he was eighteen months old. He went to early intervention school then he entered into the public school system at the age of three. When the big yellow bus pulled up in front of our house for that first time, Ryan got the biggest grin on his face I've ever seen. He whooped and hollered and flapped his arms so hard that I thought he was going to take off! As I put him on that bus, I cried and he laughed. And still to this day, he goes ecstatic when the bus comes to get him. In fact, if his sisters' bus comes first, he gets mad and throws a fit!

## Christmas Tradition

Every Christmas since Ryan has been mobile; we've had to anchor our tree to the wall. He always comes up to the tree and shakes it! He shakes it until ornaments go flying across the room hitting the walls, windows, the floor, and once in a while they have even hit me. But I've learned to dodge them now. Without fail, since he's been six years old he can and will pull or push the tree over. One particular Christmas season, we were on our way out the door to meet some friends. As we headed out to start loading the van, our dog initiated the tree. Then Ryan proceeded to pounce on the tree knocking it over. Ryan grabbed onto the tree and wouldn't let go! His Dad had to pry him off of it! He was insistent on hugging the tree. He ended up with a mouth full of fir needles. This event occurs at least once during our holiday season. Once the tree hits the ground, he claps and flaps like he's won a prize. So as you can imagine, by Christmas day our tree looks pretty ragged. Broken glass ball ornaments, (we are switching to plastic, resin, and hard dough ornaments), are stuck in between the branches because we can't find the hooks (they must've flown off when the tree was shaken) to hang them from and our tree is full of smashed branches with sagging lights with fir needles all over the carpet! Oh well, the season goes on...

## Family Field Trip

Shelby Farms is a wide expansive park in Memphis, Tennessee close to where we live. Shelby Farms has lakes, walking trails, many playgrounds, and picnic areas. One day, my husband, had this bright idea to take the three youngest kids and our three dogs to the park. So off we went. We looked like a bunch of sardines cramped in our family vehicle and I felt a little like the Griswolds from 'National Lampoons Vacation' movie. When we arrived, I got out of the truck first, taking two of the dogs. Two of Ryan's sisters got out and Todd said he'd walk with Ryan and take the last dog. As the dogs walked me down the hill, my girls followed. As I was trying to control the two dogs I had, I heard Todd start yelling and screaming, 'No!' I turned around in time to see Ryan heading straight for the closest lake. He resembled a deranged drunk as he ran down the hill. Todd ran as fast as he could to catch up with Ryan, too late. He dropped the dog leash so he could grab Ryan and into the lake went our third dog. And then in went Todd. I couldn't help him because the dogs that I had were too big to hand over to the girls at that time. So I was stuck holding the dogs. There Todd was with his shorts soaking wet with water running down his legs, he had Ryan under one arm and the dog under the other. He came stomping out of the lake and we laughed. Ryan was flapping his arms and laughing as loud as he could!
The lesson learned: we will never try that again!

## Life's Simplicities I Took for Granted

Breathing without someone sitting on my stomach, bathing alone and bathing naked, eating without dodging corn on the cob, eating food that doesn't have fingers in it, sleeping without someone sitting on my head and pounding my bottom, potty training and having success, vomit free carpets, poop free carpets, and pee free carpets, lockless refrigerators, hallways free of gates and other parent traps, conversations in English with people over 4.5 feet tall, and dinners out with my low maintenance children.

## Sleepless in Collierville

Ryan's brain doesn't naturally produce melatonin for his brain to go into sleep mode. We've tried numerous sleep agents including melatonin. Each medication only helps for a few nights and then Ryan and I are back to being awake for hours on end. Many nights I awake with Ryan sitting on top of me laughing and hitting me in the head as if to be saying, 'Mommy, get up! It's time to play!' At times, he sits on my stomach or if I'm lying on my stomach, he'll sit on top of my bottom. And I'll wake up and he'll be having the time of his life slobbering all over me. Praise God for His grace to get me through the days with out much sleep. Going without much sleep used to not affect me as much. People would tell me they couldn't tell the difference between the nights when I got six hours of sleep compared to none. I was chipper pretty much all of the time. But as I'm getting older, I'm starting to become grumpier, or so I am told. Ryan knows how to turn on his TV. And many times I'll wake up to a blaring Veggie Tales® tape singing "we are the pirates who don't do anything..." If he comes out of his room, he will also turn on *all* the lights upstairs and then work his way downstairs. I pray that one day he will sleep like a typical child.

## Antics

Ryan is notorious for getting cheese out of the refrigerator and throwing it at me or eating it wrapper and all. So now, we have a refrigerator with a lock on its handles.

When Ryan eats I have to monitor him closely or he'll eat until he vomits. But the good news is when he vomits at least we know he's finished.

We also have to watch him closely when we go to the mall or another public place. Ryan will get up out of his chair if he's not fastened in correctly. Once he's loose, he'll proceed to sit on anyone's lap. He looks around as if to case the joint for an innocent looking unsuspecting soul on whom he can pounce. Then he gets up and quickly and unsurely stumbles into their lap. I can't count how many times I've apologized to frightened strangers while I'm trying to pry Ryan off of their laps!

## Flying Corn

One summer night, we were trying to eat at the dinner table as a family and carry on a somewhat sane conversation. Bravely, I took a chance and gave Ryan a piece of corn on the cob on which to gnaw. Sounds harmless enough doesn't it? Well, in the middle of dinner, as we were talking, out of the corner of my eye I saw a yellow thing go sailing past me. I glanced up in time to see Todd dodge a hurled piece of corn on the cob. Ryan must have a good throwing arm! The corn dented the wall behind Todd's head. Object lesson: when Ryan has corn, clear out of the kitchen!

# 1ˢᵗ Corinthians 13 Ryan's Version

I can answer the same questions over and over about why Ryan can't talk yet and why he walks like a drunk man--but if I don't have love than I am just as irritating as those questions. I can recite scripture for sanity and strength all day long, have the most sanitized house in the neighborhood, the most manicured lawn on the block--but if I don't have love, I am nothing. Love is patient while cleaning up Ryan's poop. Love is kind when Ryan slaps me in head while changing his diaper. It does not envy my neighbor's typical 9 year old son who plays baseball, football, and soccer, but trusts the Lord to provide Ryan with what he needs. Love does not brag when other parents share their pain and struggles and love rejoices when other parent's children are healed. It doesn't boast, when a friend calls to whine about her tiring day with 2 typical children when I've had an exhausting day with 3 typical children and 1 handicapped child. Love is not rude when a neighbor or my husband asks, 'what have I done all day?'

It does not seek after glory when Ryan actually poops in the potty, but keeps encouraging him to do it again. It is not easily angered when Ryan tips over the Christmas tree and breaks all of my glass ornaments, for the third time. It does not delight in evil and is not self righteous when my husband doesn't listen when I say do not feed Ryan or he will throw up, and he does and vomit happens, but love rejoices in truth. Love does not give up hope when Ryan receives a discouraging medical diagnosis and prognosis. It always trusts God to protect Ryan during the day even if he can't tell me what happened. It perseveres through uncontrollable bloody noses, grand mal seizures, numerous emergency room trips, countless sleepless nights, and chopped off fingers. Love never fails. But where there are thousands of memories of sanitizing the house after Ryan paints with poop, endless days in the hospital, hundreds of doctor visits, they will fade away. Where there is unsuccessful testing and unmet goals, they will cease. Where there are phone calls from school telling me to come get Ryan, 'rebathe' him, and bring him back to start

the day over again, there will be Someone Who knows I did my best. For I know I fail all of my children and I pray they don't end up on Oprah, but when I get to heaven my failures will cease to exist. When I was a special needs child (still am and aren't we all?) I needed a parent to help me with my disabilities. Now that I'm a parent of a child that's differently abled, I need a Father who lovingly puts up with all my handicaps. And now these three remain: faith, hope, and love. But the greatest of these is love.
God loves me the way I am but loves me too much to leave me the same.

## What Did I Do All Day?

I finally got tired of a neighbor asking me, "so what do you do all day anyway?" Here is my response:

The Day in the Life of 'just a stay at home' wife and mother:

2:00 am: awake to Ryan, my 9 year old special needs son laughing and screaming

2:15 am: go into room to check on 9 year old son, he's now turned on the TV

2:30 am: go downstairs, grab sleep medication, fix a drink and snack for Ryan, the 9 year old son

2:35 am: go back upstairs, change Ryan's diaper, give him his snack and sleep medication, and beg him to please go back to sleep

3:00 am: notice that he is quiet and go check on him, he's asleep

3:01 am: turn off the TV, go to the bathroom, and climb back into bed beside snoring hubby

3:15 am: just about to fall asleep, hubby is now awake and wants some attention

3:35 am: go downstairs and get a drink

3:37 am: go back upstairs and climb back into bed and try and relax

3:50 am: last time I looked at the clock as I shut my eyes

4:00 am: awake to the sound of a blaring TV in Ryan's room

4:01 am: hear sound of approaching laughter and sagging diaper coming toward my room

4:02 am: pull covers over my head as Ryan sits on top of me trying to find out where I went

4:05 am: get tired of being climbed on, take squealing Ryan back into his room, turn down his TV, turn off his lights, and close his door

4:10 am: climb back into bed

4:15 am: close my eyes

4:30 am: youngest child, Hannah comes in and taps me on the head saying she can't go back to sleep

4:35 am: after debating with her, let her climb into bed with us

21

4:45 am: realize that I can't sleep when Hannah's elbow keeps ending up in my chest

4:47 am: get out of bed quietly as not to disturb snoring hubby, sleeping beauty and go downstairs

4:50 am: ask God what my purpose is again, and straighten office area

5:00 am: start laundry

5:05 am: sit down to read God's Word

5:15 am: hear loud laughter again and Ryan's door bursts open

5:20 am: hear hubby who was sleeping yell at Ryan

5:25 am: hear hubby get out of bed, take Ryan back into his room and slam door shut

5:26 am: ask God same question again

5:30 am: change out laundry loads

5:35 am: hear oldest daughter get up to take shower, clean downstairs bathroom, and dust

6:00 am: change out laundry loads again, unload dishwasher, open blinds, and hear hairdryer going

6:30 am: hear Ryan clomping downstairs; intervene as he almost breaks a lamp

6:33 am: change Ryan's diaper, turn around to grab wipes, as he grabs poop

6:34 am: grab hands and wipes at same time trying to hold Ryan down while cleaning his hands off, he flings his arms and sends poop flying all over me, tell Sarah to hurry up for school

6:35 am: say goodbye to oldest daughter, Sarah as she goes to high school

6:36 am: finally get Ryan's diaper changed; head upstairs to give Ryan a bath and myself a shower

6:40 am: step out of shower, put the plug back into the tub as Ryan as thrown it out letting most of the water out

6:45 am: notice that Ryan has pooped in the tub and that he is hurling it as if he were in a poop tossing contest

6:46 am: ask God same question again, while getting out of the shower and being hammered with poop

6:47 am: change out bath water, start cleaning up poopy mess, and give Ryan another bath

7:00 am: get back into shower, rewash hair and body

7:02 am: get out of shower, replug the tub, and dry off

7:03 am: get dressed
7:05 am: take pants back off so I can get into bath tub and lift Ryan out of the tub
7:10 am: still trying to get Ryan out of the tub
7:11 am: Dry off Ryan, put pants back on, and take Ryan into his room
7:13 am: diaper and dress Ryan and go back downstairs to get his daily seizure medication
7:14 am: hear TV blaring again
7:15 am: ask God same question, go back upstairs, give Ryan his meds, turn down the TV again
7: 18 am: collect more dirty laundry from 4 bedrooms, trudge back down stairs
7: 20 am: change out laundry loads
7:30 am: answer phone, listen to various questions, give advice, pray, start breakfast
7: 35 am: go back upstairs, wake up middle child, Jessica who is still in bed, wake up Hannah and check on Ryan
7:40 am: go back downstairs throw out burnt eggs, start breakfast over, change out laundry, answer phone, answer various questions, give advice, pray, discover that I forgot to start dryer
7:45 am: go back upstairs to reawake girls
7:47 am: restart breakfast again, hear stomping coming closer downstairs
7:50 am: stop arguing between the sisters and finish up breakfast
7:51 am: listen to complaining about that's not what they wanted for breakfast
7:55 am: clean up kitchen
8:00 am: go back upstairs, wake up hubby, and notice that Ryan has fallen back asleep
8:02 am: answer hubby's question, what's that smell?
8:05 am: go downstairs, check weather, answer phone, answer various questions, give advice, pray, ask God same question again, and go back upstairs and wake up Ryan
8:10 am: still trying to get Ryan to wake up
8:15 am: hear Ryan's bus pull up and drag him downstairs fighting him all the way, yell at girls to get to their bus stop

8:18 am: put Ryan on the bus, breathe a sigh of happy relief, wave goodbye as they pull off for school, and realize that still I love him

8:20 am: yell at kids at bus stop to stop fighting, wave goodbye as the girls' bus pulls up to the stop, kiss hubby goodbye and pray together

8:22 am: watch bus as it leaves to take the girls to school, wave goodbye to hubby, and hurry inside hearing the phone ringing

8:23 am: answer phone, answer various questions like, 'how do you do it?' and 'are you busy?', give advice, and promise to start writing the next A.S.K. Bible Study, change out laundry, and check email

8:30 am: official work day begins, work on Nursery schedule, return phone calls regarding the Nursery, and work on 2 year old curriculum

8:45 am: answer phone, answer various questions like, 'do you have a minute', agree to send in craft supplies and snacks for Friday's lesson, continue to work on Nursery stuff

9:30 am: run household and Nursery errands.

9:35 am: answer cell phone, answer questions like, 'what are you doing?' and 'where are you?', while driving and cutting off people in traffic

9:45 am: arrive to church, check on Nursery rooms, refill necessities, then shop for Nursery needs, household needs and get gas

10:00 am: answer cell phone again, answer questions 'do you have anything to do today?', promise to get neighbor's mail, continue to shop

10:15 am: answer cell phone again, answer questions like 'can you baby-sit?' and keep from getting sarcastic when told 'since you're at home and don't have anything else to do can you (fill in the blank)?', promise to watch for UPS man at another neighbor's house and to sign for a package, continue to shop

11:30am: stop at home, check emails, put groceries away and unload Nursery items

12:00 pm: stop by neglected friend's home for lunch

12:30 pm: answer cell phone, apologize for being rude, and promise to call the caller back when you get home, counsel friend over lunch

12:45 pm: cell phone rings again, check the number, ignore cell phone because it's not a school calling

1:00 pm: finally turn cell phone on silent, continue counseling friend

1:30 pm: head back home, get caught in traffic, and return missed cell phone calls

1:45 pm: arrive home, listen to messages, check emails, and change out laundry loads, vacuum

2:00 pm: start working on MOPS stuff

2:18 pm: realize that I'm late picking up Sarah from high school, save MOPS info

2:20 pm: rush to get Sarah, see that she has invited friends for me to take home also

2:50 pm: finish taking her friends home, return to my home

2:51 pm: go to bathroom as phone starts ringing again

2:55 pm: sit down to spend needed time with Sarah

3:20 pm: Sarah finishes homework, goes out side, and I change out laundry loads

3:30 pm: fall asleep on couch

3:40 pm: answer phone, answer why I didn't call them back yet, switch over and answer why I hadn't called them back yet

3:45 pm: Ryan's bus arrives

3:47 pm: fix Ryan a drink, snack, and change diaper

3:48 pm: the girls' bus arrives

3:50 pm: start girls on homework

3:55 pm: threaten girls and ask God that same question again

4:00 pm: wrestle with Ryan to get him upstairs, and give him a bath, let phone ring

4:03 pm: replug bath tub

4:05 pm: replug bath tub

4:06 pm: answer phone, answer various questions as 'are you busy?' smell and hear that Ryan is throwing poop again

4:07 pm: change out bath water, scold Ryan, listen to Ryan squeal as I clean poop off my glasses, and myself, clean off walls, sinks, mirror, the sides of the tub, carpet and rerun tub water

4:10 pm: replug bath tub, let phone ring, and yell downstairs to stop arguing

4:15 pm: start to get Ryan out of tub

4:20 pm: take off my pants, step into tub, lift up Ryan, and struggle to get him out of tub

4:21 pm: feel warmth on my feet realizing Ryan has just peed on me and the carpet while getting his diaper

4:22 pm: wipe Ryan off, put on his diaper (not on myself, on Ryan), dress Ryan, and change my clothes since I'm wet from getting Ryan out of the tub

4:25 pm: go downstairs threaten to hurt children if they don't stop arguing, change out laundry, answer phone

4:26 pm: tell hubby that all is well, calm, and peaceful

4:28 pm: make girls go outside, call them back inside to put up their books, backpacks, shoes, and clean up kitchen from their snacks

4:30 pm: go back upstairs, check on Ryan, and turn down blaring TV

4:35 pm: go back downstairs, start dinner, go back upstairs, check on Ryan, put a new diaper back on Ryan as he has taken his off

4: 40 pm: go back downstairs, check on dinner, change out laundry, answer phone, tell girls to go back outside, hear obnoxious screaming coming down the stairs

4:45 pm: grab Ryan as he runs into kitchen and grabs a whole loaf of bread, molding it into something of a prehistoric sort, grab his hands, and remove him from kitchen as he hits me

4:46 pm: put up gates and blockades to kitchen

4:50 pm: continue dinner, answer phone again, ask God that same question, smell poop

4:55 pm: clean up new sofa, coffee table, walls, and Ryan

5:00 pm: trying to head back upstairs for another bath while sliding down a few stairs and struggling with Ryan every step of the way as he's wiping poop all over me, finally get upstairs and Ryan undressed and into bathtub

5:05 pm: smell dinner burning; hear Hannah yelling that the dinner is burning on the stove

5:10 pm: go back downstairs, restart dinner, shoo Hannah out of the kitchen, go back upstairs, check on Ryan, replug the tub and refill water

5:15 pm: go back downstairs, answer phone, explain why you haven't called them back yet, and finish up dinner

5:20 pm: go back upstairs, take off my pants, get in tub, lift Ryan up and out of tub, diaper and redress him, change my clothes again, and carry down another load of laundry

5:30 pm; change out laundry loads, call girls in for dinner

5:35 pm: go back upstairs and check on Ryan, turn TV down again and change out video tape

5:37 pm: go back downstairs, call girls in for dinner again, reheat dinner

5:40 pm: call girls in for dinner, answer phone, feed dog, hear Ryan coming back downstairs, fix Ryan a drink

5:45 pm: tell girls to stop arguing

5:46 pm: tell girls to stop arguing

5:47 pm: tell girls to stop arguing

5:50 pm: send Jessica upstairs to finish homework and to put away clean laundry

6:00 pm: clean up kitchen; tell Hannah the first time to go upstairs to take a shower

6:05 pm: send Sarah upstairs to put away her clean laundry

6:10 pm: tell Hannah second time to get upstairs to take a shower

6:11 pm: notice that Ryan isn't downstairs anymore, gather his clean laundry, go upstairs to check on him and put away his laundry

6:12 pm: enter his room only to be beamed in the side of the face with a basketball

6:13 pm: cry, try to find my glasses as Ryan is climbing on top of my back screaming and flapping his arms

6:14 pm: still thinking Ryan will get off my back

6:15 pm: sit up with Ryan still leaching me, put away his laundry, and sit down to allow him to climb all over me

6:16 pm: yell at girls to stop arguing

6:17 pm: yell at Hannah to get into the shower, get wet, wash with the bar of soap (her entire body) rinse off under the shower, wash all of her hair, rinse it out under the shower, turn off the water, get out, and use her towel only.

6:25 pm: move Ryan off my lap, check on Hannah, hear water running and open the bathroom door to tell her to stop dancing naked in the mirror and get into the shower, and repeat the previous statements

6:30 pm: go back downstairs and check emails

6:31 pm: yell at Sarah and Jessica to stop arguing

6:32 pm: answer phone, 'No I'm not busy.'

6:40 pm: go back upstairs, check on Hannah and Ryan. Replace Ryan's diaper again and change his shirt as he has slobbered down the front, change out videos

6:45 pm: tell Hannah to hurry up and tell Jessica the first time to get a shower when Hannah is done

6:50 pm: go back downstairs, check voicemail and listen to 3 new messages from the past 10 minutes

7:00 pm: go back upstairs, make sure Hannah is in her room ready for bed, and Jessica's in the shower, collect the days' dirty laundry from Jessica and Hannah

7:03 pm: go back downstairs, change out laundry loads, answer phone, and explain why I haven't returned their calls yet

7:05 pm: go back upstairs, read to Hannah, pray, answer any questions she has, and bless her good night

7:35 pm: check on Ryan, pray over him, give Ryan his night medicine, Praise God, and go back downstairs

7:40 pm: change out laundry loads, start dishwasher, empty trash

8:00 pm: go back upstairs, tell Jessica and Sarah to stop arguing, tuck in Jessica and pray with her, and go to bathroom

8:02 pm: stomp up the stairs to get on to the girls for stomping up the stairs, yell at girls to stop yelling

8:15 pm: go back downstairs to change out laundry, go back upstairs, and give Sarah and J more clean clothes to put away

8:30 pm: pray with Jessica and tuck her in again, check on Ryan

8:35 pm: go back downstairs, work on unfinished MOPS and Nursery stuff, answer phone, and tell them, 'No I'm not busy.'

8:40 pm: click over to other phone line, tell hubby, 'I'm glad he's on his way home,' click back over, answer questions, give advice, click over, solve problem, click back over, pray with person, click back over to another call and solve problem.

9:00 pm: continue to work on Nursery stuff, MOPS stuff, hubby walks in

9:01 pm: answer phone, 'Yes I'm still awake.'

9:02 pm: sit down with hubby and answer the question: what did I do today?

9:05 pm: go back upstairs, tell Sarah it's bedtime, tuck her in and pray, check on Ryan and see that he's asleep, Hannah's asleep, tell Jessica to 'stop giggling it's time for lights out.'

9:15 pm: go back downstairs, finish up Nursery stuff, MOPS stuff, return emails, listen to new messages left while I was upstairs, and ask Todd why he didn't answer the phone

9:30 pm: change out laundry, finish answering any new emails in the past few minutes, and return calls to people whom I know are still awake

10:00 pm: yell upstairs to Sarah again it's time for bed

10:30 pm: put in last loads of laundry in washer and dryer

10:35 pm: answer phone, give counseling, pray

11:00 pm: apologize to hubby for being on the phone while he is home, go upstairs to get a bath, weigh the pros and cons of picking rice in a rice patty or living in the States

11:30 pm: climb into bed, read, Praise God, ask God that same question again, give hubby undivided attention

12:00 midnight: go back downstairs, get drinks for both of us, go back upstairs, climb back into bed, and talk with hubby about weekend plans

12:20 am: lights off

1:30 am: wake up, go downstairs, and work on A.S.K. Bible Studies

2:40 am: hear Ryan's laughter once again and the day begins again...

## Fully Depending on God

During one of the many days of feeling frustrated with Ryan, the Lord quietly spoke to my heart and pointed out that as Ryan is to me, I am to be to Him. Ryan is a word picture of what I am supposed to be. Just like Ryan depends on me to feed him, I need to depend on God's Word for nourishment. I change Ryan's dirty diapers and always give Ryan baths. God cleans up messes I make and He washes me in His Word so I'll be clean. Ryan depends on me to speak for him as I should depend on Him to speak for me and through me.   Since, Ryan doesn't talk, he indeed listens more than he speaks, hence; the two ears and one mouth theory. Ryan depends on me to dress him. I need to be dressed and clothed in the fruit of the spirit and put on the full armor of God. Ryan depends on me fully. I need to depend on God fully. Even though Ryan is handicapped in some ways physically and mentally, his spirit is whole and perfect. I've never looked at Ryan the same since that moment. He has become my model of who I strive to be in God.

## As Unto Jesus

One day, after changing several of Ryan's, stinky diapers, my frustration level was running high. I was in tears and my strength was sapped trying to lift ninety five pounds of Ryan up off the floor so I could slide the diaper underneath him. I weigh nearly one hundred eight pounds and lifting a ninety five pound boy can be quite challenging. I was complaining to God that this was a waste of my time and asked Him what lesson I should be learning through all of this. I would often ask God what my reward would be for doing this gross task and why it was dealt to me to complete. And I went on about how life wasn't fair that I had to change diapers on a nine year old boy who if typical would be well potty trained by age two or three. I was having one of my master whining ceremonies with God. During one of my pity party moments a verse came to mind. Matthew 25:40 KJV "...Verily I say unto you, insomuch as ye have done it unto the least of these...ye have done it unto me." Since then, I have no longer complained about doing anything for Ryan.

## Moments like These

One day while shopping at the local Target®, we were standing in line waiting to check out. When I heard Ryan eating something, I turned around and looked to what he was munching. He had grabbed a handful of popcorn from a lady standing in line behind us. Thank goodness that she responded with laughter.

One day at a local Burger King®, I decided that we would be driving through from now on. We had gone inside so I could let the children play after a morning of errands. As we entered into the playground area, I had to hold Ryan's hands as we walked to our seats just to make sure he didn't steal anyone's food. We were sitting there eating when Hannah, Ryan's younger sister, got stuck inside the ball pit. I would have to climb inside the ball pit and rescue her. Ugh! So I did my parental duty and climbed inside and helped her out of the pit. Just as I was climbing out, I heard children yelling and crying. What happened? Ryan had taken a sampling of all the children's French fries in the play area.

Each summer Ryan attends summer school. The bus picks him up at our house around seven in the morning and brings him home around noon. This one particular day, I put Ryan on the bus as usual. At about seven thirty I got a phone call from the county transportation department. They told me that Ryan had an accident on the bus and they needed to bring him home. I immediately started praying that he was all right. I had no clue what I was about to see. The bus returned around eight o'clock. As soon as the bus doors opened, the odor coming off the bus was enough to knock anyone off of their feet! Ryan had pooped. Not only did he poop, he played in it, painted with it, ate it, and flung it all over the bus and the bus assistant! I felt sorry for the other students on the bus. I cleaned up Ryan but I wonder who had the privilege of cleaning up that bus?

## Quick Draw McRyan

One morning at a local Cracker Barrel®, we were brave enough to *try* eating out. My husband, Todd, warned the unsuspecting waitress about Quick Draw McRyan and how fast he was at grabbing things. Todd told her that when she returned not to set anything down on the table within Ryan's reach. But she didn't listen. She brought us our drinks and set the tray right down in front of him! Ryan cleared all of them off the tray in one second flat sending ice cubes into the laps of several other customers! Gratefully, none of them were upset. Apparently, they had been observing Ryan long enough to know something was obviously different about him.

Another day during lunch hour, some other mothers and I went to our local O'Charley's® restaurant. We sat down and the server brought us our menus. At that same time, another server was walking through the aisle. I was glancing through the menu when I caught Ryan out of the corner of my eye snatching the red onion slices off the tops of three salads that were on top of the server's tray with one fail swoop. He flung the onions off his hands and squealed with triumph. The rest of the salads remained unscathed and the server never knew that Ryan had snatched the red onions off the tops of them.

## Full of *It*

Recently, I took the girls and Ryan to the mall. This is never a headache free trip. In the beginning, this trip seemingly went off without a hitch. The girls didn't argue the whole forty minute trip as they usually do. We remembered to bring Ryan's modified wheelchair. I had remembered Ryan's backpack complete with diapers, drinks, and snacks. And I managed to find a handicapped space available. This was going *too* smoothly. After parking, I finagled the chair out of the trunk of our car and his sister, Sarah, and I picked him up and placed him snuggly inside the chair and buckled him in tightly. After about a half hour perusing through the mall, I noticed that Ryan had wet his diaper. So we found a dressing room and I went in and changed him. I thought, 'no big deal'. About thirty minutes later, Ryan did it again. So we went back into the same dressing room and I changed his diaper again. Then about (you guessed it) another half hour goes by and he had wet so much that it went through his diaper and got his pants wet. So I wheeled him into a family restroom inside Sears® to change his diaper for a third time. I discovered that I had forgotten to pack more than three. I had thought since we were only going to be away for a short time that I wouldn't need anymore diapers than what I already had in his backpack. So I put a clean pair of pants on him *without* a diaper. I thought to myself since he just wet, for the third time, that he wouldn't go again until after we arrived home. After all, all we had to do now was to pay for our items and leave. Well, I was dead wrong! As we were leaving the store, he managed to leave a trail of urine from the restrooms through the children's section, shoe department, and the men's' department of Sears.

## Why Me?

I used to ask God all the time, "Why me?" It sounded so whiney; I decided not to ask that anymore; especially after a specific time of pitching a fit to the Lord about why I had been chosen to be Ryan's mom. "It's not fair!" I declared. "Why did I have to have a handicapped child? What did I do to have this happen to me?" And a still small voice whispered, "You didn't do anything to have Ryan happen to you. You were specially chosen because I knew you would care for Him the way I needed someone to take care of him. I have equipped you with My patience and My grace one needs to be a special needs parent. He is a very special child; in fact, he's one of My favorites." After that moment, the question of "Why me?" has never crossed my mind or lips again. That question has been replaced with "Why not me?"

## Who's Who?

Ryan cannot talk. So when something appears to be wrong with him, I make many trips to the local emergency room. We've been there so many times, they know us by name. During one of those routine trips, my fourteen year old daughter, Sarah accompanied us. Usually as soon as we arrive, we're immediately escorted back into a room. The doctor comes in, asks me the usual questions concerning Ryan, leaves to make a diagnosis, and returns with instructions and medication. This time was no different except, the doctor came in and looked at me then looked at my daughter and asked, "Which one of you is the Mom?" Immediately my frown went to a smile and her smile to a frown. I think I'll continue to take her everywhere I go.
Verse: A merry heart doeth good like a medicine. Proverbs 17:22 KJV

Another time, we were at that same hospital and a nurse stopped Sarah in the hall and asked her, "Honey, is your baby here?" She answered, "No, my brother is!" She has decided that she doesn't like going with me anymore.

## Word Picture

One particular day I was mopping the floor and cleaning the bathrooms. My usual weekly routine was as mundane as ever until the still small voice of Jesus uttered a word into my spirit. As I was cleaning the mirrors trying to get every spot, fingerprint, and toothpaste splatter off the bathroom mirror, I realized that this is what He does to me. He washes me, cleans me, purifies me, looks me over and does it again if necessary. He clearly wants to see His reflection in me without spot, blemish, or smudge. One thing that God has done for me by being Ryan's mom is purified my heart, attitudes, and thoughts.

To keep my housework from being boring, I have changed my entire house cleaning products to ones with uplifting names. For example, I buy Joy® dish washing liquid. When I see the name Joy, I think of the scripture, "The joy of the Lord is my strength." I use Cheer® laundry detergent. When I see that name I think of the verse when Jesus said, "be of good cheer, I have overcome the world." I think if *He* can overcome the world, *I* can overcome my laundry! Another one I use is Glad® trash bags. So when I'm taking out the trash, I think of, "This is the day that the Lord has made, I will rejoice and be glad in it." These are just a few of them I have around the house. If I told you all of the ones I use, it would take too long to write down!

## Medical Diagnosis

The fall of 2002, I had noticed that Ryan was regressing in accomplishments that he had once triumphed over. He started having frequent seizure activity and went back to crawling quite a bit. I sought his neurologist's advice. So on December 19$^{th}$, 2002, Ryan was admitted to the hospital for a routine MRI. Since Ryan's body doesn't respond appropriately to local anesthesia, he has to be (pardon the expression) 'put to sleep' for any tests to be done. Reality hit me the next day when two neurologists, one neurosurgeon, and one pediatrician, all concurred that Ryan's brain was shrinking. His brain had inoperable cysts in it that were filled with fluid. When the news came, the humorous side of me thought about making a movie called, "The Incredible Shrinking Brain," or "Honey, Ryan Shrunk His Brain." If I didn't have a sense of humor, I believe I would've lost it emotionally. I was told that they didn't have any clue of how long Ryan would be with us here on this Earth. It could be days, weeks, months, or years. As I sat there digesting the words I had heard I heard another voice in my spirit. He said, 'He wants to see Ryan healed even more than I do. He loves Ryan even more than I do.' I saw how difficult it was for Him to restrain and *not* to heal Ryan on my terms. But it is for *His* glory that Ryan is the way he is. I am walking out the truth that "Father knows best" for my life as well as Ryan's and to trust Him in everything, that His ways are higher than my ways and His thoughts are above my thoughts. He had the exact number of days calculated that Ryan would be on this earth, even *before* Ryan was born. Ryan is fulfilling the exact purpose that he is destined to fulfill. Whether or not I see the manifestation of Ryan's healing doesn't mean that he won't be whole, healthy, and healed. If it's here during this season of Ryan's life that his physical and mental state is made totally whole or if it's in heaven at Christ's feet, it will happen nonetheless. Our spirits are whole and the same size no matter how small or big we are physically. With Ryan, that is also true. He is a spirit being, who lives inside a body that possesses a soul containing his mind, will and emotions. Just because Ryan's soul and body are handicapped, doesn't mean his spirit is. So Ryan's miracle prognosis is that I know one day Ryan will be leaping and dancing for joy and talking my ears off! How do I know? I have *His* word on it! Isaiah 53:5 ...by *His* stripes *I am healed.*

## To All Parents

I'll lend you for a little while a child of mine, He said.
For you to love while he lives and mourn when he is dead.
It may be six or seven years or twenty two or three
But will you until I call him back take care of him for Me?
He'll bring his charms to gladden you and shall his stay be brief
You'll have his lovely memories as solace for your grief.
I cannot promise he will stay as all from earth return
But there are lessons taught down there I want this child to learn.
I've looked the wide world over in search for teachers true
And from the throng's that crown life's lanes I have selected you.
Now will you give him all your love~~~
Not think the labor vain nor hate Me when I come to call him back again.
I fancy that I heard them say, "Dear Lord thy will be done."
For all the joy this child shall bring the risk of grief we'll run.
We'll shower him with tenderness and love him while we may
And for the happiness we've known, forever grateful stay.
And should the angels call for him much sooner than we planned
We'll brave the bitter grief that comes and try to understand.
(Author unknown)

## Inspiring Songs

Besides God's Word, friends, and simple faith, there are a couple of songs that get me through times like these and they remind me of my focus.

### THE VALLEY SONG
Words and music by Aaron Sands, Dan Haseltine, Charlie Lowell, Stephen Mason,and Matt Odmark (C) 2003 Innocent Smith/ASCP )adm. by The Loving Company)/Bridge Building Music, Inc. /Pogostick Music (BMI). All rights administered by Brentwood-Benson Music Publishing, Inc. All rights reserved. Used by permission.

### Word of God Speak
©2002 MercyMe Exclusive marketing and manufacturing by M2 Communications LLC. 512 Autumn Springs Ct. Suite C, Franklin, Tn 37067.Distributed by Word Entertainment, An AOL Time Warner Company. Used by permission. International Copyright Secured. All rights reserved.

### He's My Son
Written and Sung by Mark Schultz

Ryan with big brother Matt.

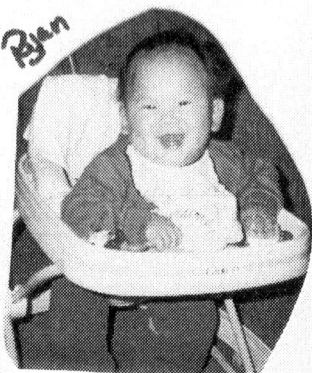
Ryan

Dad and Ryan

Baby sister, Hannah, with Ryan ↓

First haircut

Jessica     Matt     Hannah     Sarah

Ryan

Sarah Ryan

Dad

Hannah

## Good days and Better days

People are always asking me how am I doing today? The following is my answer to anyone who would ask me how my days are. Some days are good and others are better. On the good days, I wake up to my daily routine, my mind is on Ryan's medical condition and I go through the day mechanically and I can cry at a drop of a hat. I know God is still sovereign and still in control and everything is in His hands. But my emotions are on my sleeves. During those times I don't *feel* His presence and that's when my walking by faith kicks in and not by sight. On the better days, I wake up to my schedule, my mind is on God's calling and purpose for my life and His miracle promise~ Ryan's healing, and I enjoy the day and hope. The best day would be however, to awake in heaven with Ryan running around the golden streets telling 'knock knock' jokes to Jesus and hearing them both laugh!

Things that are seen are subject to change, things that are unseen are eternal...

## Glimmers of Hope

Every once in a while with prompting and assistance, Ryan will eat with a spork. There are days when he *will* poop on the potty and *not* fling, play, or eat it. Sometimes Ryan will kiss me and make the real kissing sound too! Seldom, Ryan will help dress himself like lift his bottom up while I pull up his pants. Once, he moved his Daddy's briefcase over to his Daddy's chest of drawers. Ryan stood on top of the briefcase so he could knock everything off that was on top. Two out of three times, Ryan will climb up into the truck by himself with little or no assistance. He no longer tries to eat bugs. Often times, he will actually *not* eat sand, dirt, mulch, and rocks. With a lot of help, he will pick up a toy and place it into the toy bin. Many times Ryan will tug on my clothes and push me toward the couch in our living room and make me sit down. He will then proceed to climb up onto my lap and cuddle with me. Ryan always gives me the opportunity and privilege of kissing him by putting his face smack dab in front of mine. At times, he won't get fresh with me or my friends. Yes, even though he is handicapped, he is like a typical boy in that he does try and beep a boob. One time out of twenty, he won't grab someone else's food. Now, those are a few things for which to be thankful!

## Hold Your Breath

When Ryan migrates toward boys his size playing in our cove, I hold my breath and wonder what he is thinking. I hold my breath wondering what the other boys are thinking. There are times when they voice their opinions. Like, 'uh oh, here comes Ryan!' or 'here he comes again.' So far, only one boy has been mean to Ryan or made fun of him. But the others haven't really said a word to him. However; there is one neighbor in particular, Brett, who is twelve years old, that has taken Ryan under his wing and actually plays with him when he is outside. He comes over and swims with Ryan and tosses the ball back and forth with him. But usually when Ryan ambulates toward the group playing basketball in our cove, he just grabs their basketball, lies down on a neighbor's driveway, and licks the ball and no one says a word. They just go and get another ball.

.

## Once In a Lifetime

Ryan loves watching NASCAR racing on television. So Todd thought Ryan would love to go to Talladega, Alabama to see the Aaron's 312 Busch Series Race. Against my better judgment I allowed this to happen. The race started at noon on a Saturday. So we got up and left by 4:00 in the morning to get there in time. We drove the six hours is takes to get there. And as soon as we reached the city limits of Talladega, we hit traffic; it was a dead stand still. A four lane highway had been turned into six to accommodate all the incoming NASCAR fanatics. This is *not* a place for children. We saw sights that I thought *Todd* could *only imagine*. Signs commanding certain female body parts to be flashed, raunchy port-o-potties, and drunkards were everywhere. When we finally reached the race track it was almost time for the race to start. So we parked (what seemed like) a thousand miles away from the stadium and walked as fast we could each of us holding onto one hand of stumble boy. The faster we wanted to walk, the heavier Ryan became. In fact, he actually tried slowing down so he could sit. down on the pavement. Crowds were almost unbearable. This is not a place for people with claustrophobia, agoraphobia, or xenophobia. People ran into Ryan and almost knocked him down. It's difficult trying to lug him through crowds. Once we got through the entrance, we finally found our seats and sat down. I didn't realize how hot the track would be. It was so hot that we discovered that Ryan doesn't sweat. He gets deep red all over and very dry and hot feeling. There wasn't anything I could do to cool him off. And as the cars came around, he didn't flap his arms and squeal with delight like Todd thought he would, but instead he shook with fear and hid in my side. That poor boy! The only thing that consoled him during the race was listening to the drivers' conversations with their pit crews via the race radio. He also enjoyed eating French Fries and drinking ice cold Coke®. Instead of drinking our water I brought, I used it to sprinkle on him to cool him off. Every time the cars roared around the track he'd shake and try to hide his face. It was pitiful! Once the race was over, he cooled off quite a bit as people who were above us in the bleachers emptied their coolers of beer and melted ice onto the tops of our heads. What a treat. This trip was indeed a once in a lifetime trip. Afterwards, trying to find where we parked was an adventure in itself. Todd ended up having to carry Ryan back to the truck. Once we found it, I changed Ryan's diaper and let the truck cool off before trying to drive home. Little did I know I would be cleaning up puke for six hours. On the way home, we discovered that from being in the hot sun all day, he vomits until he dry heaves. All the way back home I cleaned up half digested French Fries, Coke®, and other unidentifiable objects. He suffered from heat exhaustion or heat stroke, whichever one was more miserable. I just know that he was miserable which meant that I was miserable. Lesson learned? Don't trust your husband's instincts about your handicapped child. Just because he loves watching it on the television, doesn't mean that he will enjoy it in person. Mother knows best in this instance. Ryan has not smiled nor flapped his arms inside Alabama since that trip. This was indeed a once in a lifetime trip!

**I am the child...**

I am the child who cannot talk. You often pity me. I see it in your eyes. You wonder how much I'm aware of...I see that as well. I am aware of much...whether you are happy or sad or fearful, patient, or impatient, full of love and desire, or if you are just doing you're duty by me. I marvel at your frustration, knowing mine can be far greater, for I cannot express myself or my needs as you do. You cannot conceive my isolation, so complete it is at times. I do not gift you with clever conversation, cute remarks to be laughed over and repeated. I do not give you answers to your everyday questions, responses over my well being, sharing my needs, or comments about the world around me. I do not give you rewards as defined by the world's standards...great strides of development for which you can credit yourself. I do not have your understanding as you know it.

What I do give you is much more valuable...I give you instead opportunities. Opportunities to discover the depth of your character not mine: the depth of your love, your commitment, your patience, your abilities, the opportunity to explore your spirit more deeply than you imagined possible. I drive you further than you would ever do on your own, working harder, seeking answers to your many questions, and creating questions with no answer. I am the child who cannot talk.

I am the child who cannot walk. The world sometimes seems to pass me by. You see the longing in my eyes to get out of this chair, to run, and play like other children. There is so much you take for granted. I want the toys on the shelf. I need to go to the bathroom. Oh, I've dropped my fork again. I am dependent on you in these ways. My gift to you is to make you aware of your great fortune, your healthy back and legs, your ability to do for yourself. Sometimes people appear not to notice; I always notice them. I feel not so much envy as desire; desire to stand upright, to put one foot in front of the other, to be independent. I give you awareness. I am the child who cannot walk.

I am the child who is mentally impaired. I don't learn easily, if you judge by the world's measuring stick. What I do know is the infinite joy in the simple things. I am not burdened as you are with the strife and conflicts of more complicated life. My gift to you is to grant you freedom to enjoy as a child, to teach you how much you arms around me mean, to give you love. I give you the gift of simplicity. I am the child who is mentally impaired.

Reprinted from "Education Update," vol. 14, no. 2, Ohio Coalition for the Education of handicapped Children. Dedicated to Daryl Haynes, *The Little Boy Who Cannot Talk*.

## The Special Mother

Most women become mothers by accident, some by choice, a few by social pressures, and a couple by habit.

This year nearly 100,000 women will become mothers of disabled children. Did you ever wonder how mothers of disabled children are chosen?

Somehow, I visualize God hovering over the Earth selecting His instruments of propagation with great care and deliberation. As He observes, He instructs His angels to make notes in a giant ledger:

"Armstrong, Beth, son. Patron Saint Matthew.
Forest, Marjorie, daughter. Patron Saint Cecilia.
Rutledge, Carrie, twins. Patron Saint...hmmm, give her Gerard, he is used to profanity."

Finally, He passes a name to an angel and smiles, "Give her a disabled child." The angel is curious. "Why this one, God? She is so happy." "Exactly," smiles God. "Could I give a disabled child to a mother that does not know laughter? That would be cruel."

"But does she have patience?" asks the angel.

"I don't want her to have too much patience, or she will drown in a sea of self pity and despair. Once the shock and resentment wear off, she'll handle it."

I watched her today. She has that sense of self and independence that are so rare and so necessary in a mother. You see the child I am going to give her has his own world and that's not going to be easy."

"But, Lord, I don't think she even believes in You.' says the angel.

God smiles. "No matter, I can fix that. This one is perfect. She has just enough selfishness."

The angel gasps, "Selfishness? Is that a virtue?"

God nods and says, "If she can't separate herself from her child occasionally, she'll never survive. Yes, here is a woman whom I will bless with a child less than perfect. She doesn't realize it yet, but she is to be envied."

"She will never take for granted a spoken word. She will never consider a step ordinary. When her child says Momma for the first time, she will witness a miracle and know it. When she asks her son, who cannot talk, what his day was like, she'll learn to read facial expressions, eyes, and smiles."

"I will permit her to see clearly the things I see--- ignorance, cruelty, prejudice, and allow her to rise above them. She will never be alone. I will be at her side every minute of every day of her life because she is doing My work as surely as she is here by My side."

"And what about her patron saint?" asks the angel, his pen poised in mid air, ready to write.

God smiles, "A mirror will suffice."
(Author unknown)

## Welcome to Holland

I am often asked to describe the experience of raising a child with a disability, to try and help people who have not shared that unique experience understand it, to imagine how it would feel. It's like this: When you're going to have a baby, it's like planning a fabulous vacation trip to Italy. You buy a bunch of guide books and make your wonderful plans to see the Coliseum, Michelangelo's David, and the gondolas in Venice. You may even learn some handy phrases in Italian. It's all very exciting.

After months of eager anticipation, the day finally arrives. You pack your bags and off you go! Several hours later, the plane lands. The flight attendant comes in and says, "Welcome to Holland."

"Holland?" you say, "What do you mean Holland? I signed up for Italy! I'm supposed to be in Italy. All my life I've dreamed of going to Italy." But there's been a change in the flight plan. They've landed in Holland and there you must stay.

The important thing is that they haven't taken you to a horrible, disgusting, place full of pestilence, famine, and disease; it's just a different place. So you must go out and buy new guidebooks and you must learn a whole new language. You will meet a whole new group of people you would have never met. It's just a different place. It's slower paced than Italy, less flashy than Italy. But after you've been there awhile, and you catch your breath, you look around and you begin to notice that Holland has windmills. Holland has tulips. Holland even has Rembrandt.

But everyone else you know is busy coming and going from Italy. And they're bragging about what a wonderful time they had there. And for the rest of your life you will say, "Yes, that's where I was supposed to go, that's what I had planned." And the pain of that will never, never go away because the loss of that dream is a very significant loss. But if you spent your life mourning the fact that you didn't get to go to Italy, you may never be free to enjoy the very special, the very lovely things about Holland.

By: Emily Pearl Kingley.

## Baseball story

One Saturday, one of my neighbors took Ryan to her son's baseball game. She used to pick him up and take him quite frequently. But this one particular time, Ryan decided to show out. First they sat Ryan beside the dug out so he would feel like a part of the team. During the game, he clapped, flapped, hollered and squealed with glee. During a break, my neighbor and the coaches took Ryan up to the plate to bat. She stood behind him and held him as he held the bat. They practiced swinging a few times. Then the pitcher pitched the ball. SMACK! Ryan hit the ball! (With my neighbor's help and guidance) But nevertheless he hit it! He dropped that bat and went to clapping, flapping, and stomping. He was so excited! He was all grins. Then when the actual game restarted, Ryan became a little bit agitated because he had to sit back down on the bench. At the end of the game when the teams were giving high fives to each other, Ryan started crying. In fact he cried until real tears ran down his cheeks and he fell on the ground and wouldn't stand up. He was having a temper tantrum! He must've known it was the end of the game. My neighbor bent down, tried not to smile, and said in a stern voice, "Listen here Ryan, if you want to come back again, you're going to have stop crying, stand up, and walk with me to the van because I can't carry you." Fair enough, he immediately stopped crying, stood up, and walked to the van hand in hand with her. This shows me that he must understand much more than we give him credit. The little dickens uses his handicap many times to get his way.

The next few excerpts were written by a few friends that love Ryan.

Thank you for taking the time to write something about Ryan. It means more than words can express. I love you girls!

The moment that I will never forget about my Ryan: In the year 2002, I visited the family and as usual Ryan came to sit by me as he did others I had my hands palm down on the sofa Ryan reached over picked my hand up turned it over and gave me a high five and that instant our spirits bonded. I knew Ryan was in there saying he loved me.
Submitted by: Mrs. Page

I have never been around anyone like Ryan. Honestly, it has taken me a while to get the courage to watch him without his parents being around. The first couple of times he gave me the poop show, so that is no longer a surprise to me. Thankfully, the last time I stayed the night to watch him; he slept like a baby and even slept in. I was so surprised! Don't let Ryan fool you, as he is a smart boy. I asked him one time to pick up his cup from the floor and sure enough, he picked it right up! Many of you know Ryan has a finicky appetite, but we found out he likes my Spanish rice! Some days I can give him a fruit smoothie and other days he just spits it out. I guess sometimes his taste buds change on him. The thing that stands out the most with Ryan is the dream I had about him just recently. I had a dream that he was standing directly beside me speaking like a normal 9 year old boy! It has encouraged me and I hope it will encourage you to pray for Ryan's healing in this area!
God Bless,
Jackie Furlong

Lunchtime----snacktime---cooking activities-
Whenever and wherever that is when we see Ryan's creativity and ability to communicate the most

He began with pure determination to get the food he desired. This usually meant taking the food with his hand. It did not matter to him if it was on a neighbor's plate, napkin, or tray. If he wanted it--- he got it.

When hungry or thirsty, Ryan would cry or yell and since he did this also when he was tired, sick, or bored, we decided to concentrate on helping him communicate with us what he desired.

We began in the lunchroom and with a fork instead of his fingers. It did not take Ryan more than a few weeks to learn that using the fork enabled him to make choices and communicate wants. He would use the fork to place on top of the food he wanted to eat.

Some assistance was required to spear the food, but Ryan quickly picked up on the scooping technique. He also learned he could usually get more of a food if he wanted seconds by placing his fork on top of the empty space.

The look of satisfaction on Ryan's face spoke a thousand words. Independence, communicating with others, eating and enjoying life is what Ryan desires; just like everyone.

Our job as teachers is to try and give him the tools to make his desires a reality.

Melanie Moss: Ryan's Functional Skills Teacher

When I first met Ryan, I think I was a little afraid. I was afraid of my reaction when I met him, and afraid to really get to know him. However, this fear ended up melting away as I looked into Ryan's face. It was like looking at total innocence and love. I then had to conquer the fear of taking care of Ryan for a few hours. But that, too went away as I spent time with him as he is so easy to love.

Then there was the time that Corinne went out of town for a few days and asked if I could help watch him while she was away. At first I was a little apprehensive, but knew that I could not refuse out of my love for Corinne and Ryan. I think I was really afraid of Ryan having a seizure or some other medical emergency on my watch. I had to let go and let God be in control once again. I ended up having so much fun that night! I arrived to relieve Jackie who had been watching Ryan earlier in the day. She was letting me know what Ryan was going to eat for dinner as we were making the transition for her to leave. Little did we know that Ryan was beginning to smear his poop all over the kitchen floor and himself. Oh no!!! It was time for a bath. It took both of us to get Ryan to the top of the stairs and get his clothes off and into the tub. Ok, now what... Well, we washed him up, and then told Ryan to get out of the tub. He just grinned with that sweet grin that he has and just laid in the bottom of the tub. Now what??...At about this time we said to each other, "How in the world does Corinne do this sometimes several times in one day by herself." In the meantime, Ryan was checking us out to see if we were going to make him get out of the tub since his Mom was not there. Well we did get him out and dried off and back downstairs to finish his dinner.The rest of the evening he played with his big ball and smiled and laughed and eventually cuddled up next to me on the couch. As I looked at Ryan, I thought, this is how God looks at us. He cleans us up after we get into a big mess, but then just looks at us and smiles with His love.

I continue to learn about God's love whenever I am with Ryan and am blessed to know him. By Lynn Keller

I first met Ryan when he was 3 years old.  He couldn't walk very well, but he could shuffle anywhere he wanted to go.  His first encounter with me was to shuffle over and vomit in my lap.  This delighted him, and he laughed very much.  He enjoyed it so much, that he has done it several times since.

Once, I was rushing with his mother to take him to the hospital because of an epileptic attack when he decided to stop seizing and vomit on my lap once again.

Another time I was going to bed after watching Ryan that day, only to find he had left his trademark deposit on my pillow.  After showering a couple of times and a trip to Target to replace the "marked" pillow, I could laugh about the gift he left me.

He has vomited in my backyard, in my car, on my driveway, in my kitchen and den, and once on my husband.

One would think that this would make me run and hide when Ryan comes toward me.  Does he think that I am a toilet and it's proper to vomit on me?  Does he hate me and wish me to go away?  Do I make him sick to his stomach, literally?  Because only Ryan and God know the answer to this, I must only speculate.

Ryan's physical handicaps cause him to vomit easily.  Ryan's mental handicaps make him unable to comprehend that this is not polite behavior.  Ryan has no idea that this is improper and obviously, gross!  But in some strange way, I am honored that he feels comfortable enough around me to know that I will love him, even when he vomits.

One cannot hold another responsible for things they cannot help.  Would a parent punish a two week old for soiling a diaper?  Would someone expect a wheelchair bound child to walk to the store?  No!  I cannot hold Ryan responsible for the vomit he dearly loves to share and I will continue to clean myself up after every yucky encounter with him and his stomach contents.

What is amazing about this story is that God does the same for us. Doesn't God keep coming around us even when we shuffle up and abuse Him? He cleans Himself off and offers His arms to us, willing to continue caring for us, aching to hold us, cleaning us before we are soiled, making us presentable, and showing us unconditional love. He doesn't run and hide, even though He knows our ability to ruin the purest of things. He desires to be close because He loves us, through all of our filth. Ryan has shown me that I need to trust God to love me even when I am unable to comprehend that what I am doing is offensive to God. Knowing that most times when Ryan comes near me, he will crawl in my lap, pat my arms, and allow me to hold him and love him, makes it worthwhile. A little vomit cannot take away all the sloppy kisses and hugs I have received from this loving child. I like to think that the Heavenly Father thinks the same about me.

Sarah Kebschull

## Miracles Happen

In light of Ryan's recent diagnosis, and his multiple regressions of physical capabilities, he is still miraculously improving. For example, he has been using the potty for more than a small wading pool. He actually has gone to the restroom in the potty. He may go days in a row and many days he's not successful at it, but the key here is, he is actually sitting on it and not trying to put his feet in it or splash in it. After a successful bathroom break, he tries to grab the contents out of the potty every once in a while. But who hasn't been tempted to do that at least once in their life?

## Short and To the Point

Lately, he will accept a short, to-the-point command like, "Ryan, give me your feet so I can put your shoes on." He will stick one foot in the air while to put that shoe on and then he'll give you the other foot. He does the same thing with washing off his hands. He will give you his hands one at a time when he knows he's dirty and when he sees that you have a washcloth in your hand. One morning, I took a wipe out of his backpack and stepped toward him. He puckered his lips thinking I was going to wash off his mouth .Instead I wiped off his eyes and nose. He wasn't too happy about that! He definitely doesn't like when he mistakenly guesses incorrectly what you're going to do; especially if it involves him.

## Like Father like Son

Despite Ryan's handicaps, at times he acts like a typical boy. For example, he will start his high pitch screaming when I get on the phone. Or when we're watching a television show, he will wobble over to the TV and just turn it off! And Many times he doesn't hear me when I'm talking to him, especially when he is watching television. I will request for him to do something and he just sits there and continues to watch television. During times like these, he reminds me of his Dad.

## Showing Off

Lately, Ryan has been more alert. Despite his diagnosis and prognosis, he has been progressing quite well, and he is at the stage of mocking. He screams very shrill squeals at school when he's not getting any attention and his teacher, will get in his face and say "SHHH! Ryan, no screaming!" And *usually* he listens to her. But I try and do that and he pops me on top of the head or he says, "SHHH!" in return. Then he smiles his mischievous smile, and I melt. I have to remind myself and the girls *not* to laugh at him when he does it. I've discovered the more we laugh at him when does funny things, the more he does them.

# Fire!

One day during this past Christmas season, I was cleaning and the children were playing unusually well together. I was in the kitchen and Ryan was playing with one of his bouncy balls. As I was cleaning and singing Christmas carols, I smelled something that wasn't poop. Then I recognized it was a burning smell. I ran into the living room and noticed that Ryan's socks were smoking! He had been playing with a ball near the fireplace when he thought it would be a good idea to stick his feet into the fireplace instead. When he did, his feet caught on fire! I started yelling, "Ryan's socks are smoking!" (I never thought I'd be yelling that) The girls came running in with water and towels. But as usual he didn't feel it as we would have felt it. He has a sensory integration disorder which means he doesn't feel physical pain or textures the way we feel pain. He really likes hot water, it could burn his skin, but he wouldn't feel it. He is highly agitated when cold water touches his skin. He seems like he's in pain when cold touches him. Go figure. Also when he feels wind, he curls up in a ball and lies down on the driveway and will not move no matter how many Cheetos® are used to bribe him!

## Potty Training

I have been potty training Ryan for six years so far. In the beginning of his training he had a chair that strapped to the toilet seat that resembled an electric chair. I'd undress him, sit him on top of the seat, and fasten him in securely so he wouldn't fall off. He looked like he'd been convicted of a crime...and he had: still wearing diapers! After he was successfully strapped in, we'd wait. And wait. And wait. And many times, nothing. Sometimes I'd hear a drop and I'd praise him to high heaven. Seldom, I'd hear a plop and reward him with cheese curls or his favorite cereal.

He has outgrown the execution seat and his bottom fits quite well on top of the regular size toilet seat. Ryan will have complete potty success every once in a while. He even did it three days in a row! I would take him in the bathroom and take his pants off of him and wait as he sat there. Each time took about thirty minutes of waiting and running the faucet. But then he started trying to reach inside the bowl and grab the contents thereof. The wait got longer and longer. He still doesn't recognize that he needs to go to the bathroom when 'that feeling' comes upon him and he will still go in his diapers. Oh well...the potty training goes on!

## Forgotten Son

Every school year I have two M Team meetings with his teachers, therapists, and a school representative. An M-TEAM meeting is a meeting to decide individual goals and objectives for that particular student. Since Ryan is in Special Education, it's mandatory that we have these. He is in a Functional Skills class which he learns life's basics on how to function independently. He is learning to drink from a cup and set it down on the table when finished and not to hurl it across the cafeteria. He is also learning to eat with utensils and not to steal his neighbor's food. Other things he is being taught are: stacking blocks, simple sign language for the words: eat, drink, and more, and other skills too numerous to mention.

One afternoon there was an M-TEAM meeting scheduled to discuss goals and objectives for Ryan. I had been shopping and running errands that morning and stopped by a girlfriend's house to visit. Well, I ended up having lunch there and I casually mentioned how strange it was not to have anything planned that afternoon. So we just hung out until it was time to pick up the children at school.

I arrived that afternoon to pick up the children; I waited in the car line as usual. Ryan's teacher walked out with Ryan to put him into my van. She casually mentioned, "Hi there! We missed you at Ryan's meeting today." I had totally blown off the meeting that was scheduled in advance! I had simply forgotten! How could a mom forget her own child? Just ask a mother with three or more children, believe me it happens!

## War Zone

Recently when the Memphis area was being showered with thunderstorms, lightening, pelting rain, and hail, none of us got very much sleep. Ryan's brain doesn't produce the melatonin he needs for sleep, so he is on sleep medicine. But he usually doesn't sleep much at all so, neither do I. This particular week of night storms was even unusual for Ryan and me. Imagine at two o'clock in the morning everyone is sleeping sweetly and KABOOM! Thunder rolls and your husband nudges you and frantically asks, "What just blew up?!" You assure him it was nothing but thunder. He turns back over to go to sleep when you hear, "Yaaaa! Eeeahhhh!" A shrill scream followed by the sound of television fuzz at the loudest volume the TV can go! Then right after those, another KABOOM of thunder. So in between earth quaking thunder are Ryan's squeals, screams, and TV fuzz! It's a wonder the other children remained asleep. This continued for about four hours. Then it was time for me to get up and start the day. Ryan's dad said he dreamt we were in a war zone. I laughed because it sure did sound like one!

## Shania Twain

We have watched a lot of videos in the middle of the night but still many times Ryan is inconsolable. When Veggie Tales®, Bear and the Big Blue House®, or Jay Jay the Jet Plane® are not sufficient, we pop in *the* Shania Twain concert video. Two hours of nonstop country music. It's magic. It's a miracle. It's Shania Twain. Ryan calms right down and intently watches her and even bounces to the music. And sometimes, he'll even fall back to sleep! Ah, more rest for mom!

## Number 600

Ryan's call number at church is six hundred. He is in Bethesda, the Special Needs Nursery. The first night I left him in there, I was hesitant to say the least. This was the second time I'd tried leaving him with someone who didn't know him. But I tried. I wanted to get in to hear the Pastor preaching. So, I signed Ryan in, got his call number and went into the service. About thirty minutes into the teaching, I saw Ryan's number go up. I rushed out of the sanctuary to be met by an awful stench and one of the caregivers in his room. He had thrown poop all over the Nursery! What a nightmare! A mother's and a caregiver's! I went inside the room to clean him, the Nursery walls, toys, carpet, you name it, poop was everywhere! When I opened the door, there was Ryan smiling and giggling as loud as he could while he flapped and clapped his hands. He was extremely proud of himself and happy of his accomplishment.

## Stealth!

I am told quite frequently that Ryan is pretty sneaky and super fast. He is like a stealth fighter plane; very quick and quiet with his approach. As soon as you're not expecting it BAM! He gets you. As his mom, I have also witnessed Ryan in action thousands of times. There are two prime examples of this fact. The first one happens a lot in the school cafeteria. He will be eating his lunch, and then he'll realize he's out of his corn. While no one is looking he will borrow the corn off his neighbor's plate. His teacher will try and catch him doing this as he is very fast. She says that she'll be watching him out of the corner of her eye when ZAP! Ryan grabs the entire helping of corn from his neighbor's plate in one fail swoop onto his own plate. He continues to eat without missing a beat. Another time was recently at our house. One night, some of our friends came over for dinner. Everyone knows that you have to be quick to move when Ryan is around while you have food on your plate. So this night, we were on high alert, watching Ryan's every move. If he even looked like he thought about swiping someone's food, we'd move and we'd move quickly! Since, we had made it through dinner without a single 'food snatching incident', we relaxed in guarding our food (the wrong thing to do). As we were having dessert, chatting and laughing, Ryan's dad warned my girlfriend to beware of Ryan. He was spying on her food out of the corner of his eyes. She said, "Oh, I'm watching him. It's ok." Within two seconds of her saying that, WHOOSH! In one swift swoop, he successfully nabbed an entire piece of cake off of her plate!

## Wrestling at Midnight

Since Ryan's brain does not produce melatonin on its own, he takes sleep medication. Many times, I will forget to give it to him. Ryan does sleep but it's in small increments. If I want him or need him to sleep all night, at least six hours in a row, I give him the night time medication. This particular night, he'd fallen asleep before I could give it to him and I didn't want to wake him to give him his medication. We went up to bed as normal. Around midnight, Ryan came into our room squealing and waving his arms. He flailed himself on top of his Dad and started trying to wrestle him. Well Todd wasn't in the mood to wrestle, so he led Ryan back to his bed and closed his door. Todd got back into bed. About thirty minutes later, Ryan was back in our room again this time he's all over me! He had climbed over Todd and landed on me. He was laughing, screaming, and had a big smile on his face. So I led him back to his room, stuck in a forty-five minute video, and closed his door. I got back into bed. As I was just falling asleep, there he was again! This time, he ran and tackled Todd. Todd got up and led Ryan back to his room, put in another forty-five minute video, gave him a drink, and closed his door, and got back into bed. About an hour later, he came into our room again. This time he climbed in between us and got under the covers. I thought for sure Ryan was on the way to sleepy time land. But I was wrong, because he started cackling and trying to grab my pillow out from under my head! So, I got up led him back into his room, put in another forty-five minute video, gave him another drink, a bowl full of dry cereal, and closed his door. Then about an hour later, I was still awake waiting for him to come back into our room. I didn't hear anything, so I got up and checked on him. He was still awake but he was lying very still. So I quietly closed the door. I walked to my room, climbed into my bed, and quickly started to fall asleep. WHAM! His door came swinging open and Ryan ran out into the hallway clapping and laughing. Oh no! This time Todd woke up and got smart, too. He put in a Shania Twain video which happens to be two hours long. We didn't hear from Ryan from five o'clock until seven o'clock.

## Top Twenty

Twenty stupid things not to say to a mom
(These have actually been said to me)
1. What's wrong with him?
2. He needs to watch where he's going!?
3. He doesn't appear handicapped.
4. What's he got?
5. What's his problem?
6. What did you do during pregnancy?
7. Is it contagious?
8. I can watch the 'other' kids for you.
9. Call me if you need help.
10. If I were you, I would've committed suicide.
11. So when's he supposed to die?
12. You need to spank him when he does that.
13. Have you tried disciplining him?
14. You should discipline him.
15. What possessed you to have another kid after Ryan?
16. Weren't you scared to have another kid after Ryan?
17. Suggest when to sleep, when to do housework, and when to get work done.
18. Can't you get everything done before Ryan gets home?
19. Offer unsolicited advice unless you are walking in the same shoes.
20. I'm sorry and bless your heart.

The following are things that people have actually said or done for us. These are great things to do or say.

1. What is his diagnosis?
2. Can I help you with him?
3. Let me know what I can do to help you.
4. I can take Ryan for a night so you can rest.
5. Can I spend time with your family so I can get to know Ryan?
6. He sure is handsome!
7. It must be difficult to find a discipline that works with him.
8. Go on a family outing with us without being embarrassed.
9. Invite us over as a family. Including Ryan.
10. God sure has given grace to you.
11. Show up and take Ryan to a baseball game, the zoo, to the mall, etc.
12. Show up and help give Ryan a bath, help feed Ryan dinner, etc.
13. Watch Ryan while I help the girls with their homework.
14. Talk with Ryan's sisters and brother and find out their perspective on Ryan.
15. Take an interest in him.
16. Hold him down while I cut his fingernails or toenails or just come over and do it.
17. Offer to watch him, while I take his sisters to the mall.
18. Offer to keep him while we go on a family vacation so *we* can have a vacation.
19. Actually keep Ryan when offering to do so.
20. Pray for Ryan and our family's sanity, strength, and peace.

## How to obtain free towels

Take your son in to the emergency room while he is having seizures. As he is vomiting upon arrival, nurses will come help you by giving you a bunch of hospital towels. As you clean up the mess, they will not want those towels back but proceed to give you a plastic laundry bag to put dirty clothes and towels in once you're finished cleaning up. Thus you've acquired free towels. Ok, well they're not really free being that you have to pay for the hospital trip, but nevertheless, you've gotten your money's worth out of it!

## Dreams

I remember two dreams I had about Ryan before he walked. The dreams were the same. In each dream Ryan was walking. And each time I had that dream, his Dad had the same dreams. A couple years later, Ryan walked. He isn't the most stable of walkers, but nevertheless, he's mobile!

For the past few years, his Dad and I have had the same dreams again. Except in these dreams Ryan is talking. And he is talking in English! Not his usual babble. What's interesting about this is that I've had two girlfriends call me and tell me that they have had dreams that Ryan is talking with them. One girlfriend lives out of state, the other is local. Does this mean he'll talk before he goes home to be with Jesus? I don't know. But these dreams give me hope.

## Did Somebody Say McDonald's®?

For some strange reason Ryan was born with an innate sense of McDonalds. Every time we'd drive through or stop in to eat, he would become more alert and fidgety in his car seat. Even though he couldn't say that he wanted cheeseburgers or French Fries, he would glare at my food as I ate. When he was about two years old, he started verbalizing high pitched squeals of glee when we'd drive into a McDonald's parking lot. As time has passed, he continues to point, scream, and tries to get out of his seatbelt when he sees a McDonalds or hears the name mentioned. So everyone in our family knows NOT to say that name unless you plan on going to McDonald's to buy Ryan a cheeseburger, fries, and a drink. It doesn't matter if you're whispering the word; do not let Ryan hear you. He will holler until you take him to McDonald's and buy him that cheeseburger, fries, and drink.

Even at age nine, when we are out driving, if he sees a McDonald's he starts waving his arms and squealing gleefully. If we stop, all is well. If not, when we get home and drive into the garage without his cheeseburger, fries, and drink, he will start whining, which turns into whimpering, which turns into crying, which turns into screaming! When we do stop and get his Number Two Combo super sized, he will pat me on the shoulder when he needs or wants a bite. If I don't respond quickly enough, he resorts to hitting, smacking, or pulling my hair.

One day, I drove through the dry cleaners to pick up his Dad's clothes; he thought we were at McDonald's. We sure had a hard time convincing him that we were *not* at McDonalds!

## How to be first at the doctor's office

Bring in Ryan for his appointed time. Discover that the staff is running behind. Then discover that you've forgotten to bring snacks and a drink for Ryan. Ryan starts to give a high pitch squeal that almost shatters my glasses and everyone else's for that matter! His squeal increases to humming then to rocking and then to flapping of his arms. The nurse comes out and calls his name next even though he's fifth in line. But no one seems to mind that he was called before they were. Go figure.

## How to cut to the front of a line at Target

Make an unexpected stop at Target. Try to find a handicapped parking space, but they're all taken by cars without a handicapped sign or license tag. Find a place near the back of the parking lot. Park there and get out Ryan's oversized chair trying not to scrape the car next to yours. Then try and lift Ryan out of the car and into the chair without him wiping his hands all over the car next to yours. Once you have Ryan strapped in the chair, once again try to back the chair out of the tight squeeze between your car and the car next to yours which happens to be a beamer. (And it appears to be a new one at that.) Go into Target, do your shopping. Continue to push Ryan's chair with one hand and pull the cart behind you with the other hand without knocking any displays or merchandise over. Then when you are finished, get into the check out line that's the slowest moving. While you're in line, try and keep Ryan from grabbing anything within his reaching distance such as gum, candy, magazines, nail files, matches, toothbrushes, matchbox cars, etc. Next, hear a slight toot sound followed by a stench that you wish you didn't smell. Then notice that the three people that were ahead of you in line politely leave the line and get behind you telling you to go ahead. And that's how you cut in front of people in line at Target.

## Ryan on the loose!

One Sunday afternoon after overseeing the Nursery for two Sunday morning services, I was beat. I came home hoping to get a nap. I was so tired that I didn't change clothes, grab a bite to eat, or even set any of my church stuff down. I went straight upstairs and collapsed on my bed. My husband, Todd came up stairs and told me that he was taking the kids to Target but he was leaving Ryan here. I sighed and told him that was fine, but that I was going to sleep. He locked all the doors, put up the restraining gates to block Ryan from getting into the kitchen, and gave Ryan some cereal and a drink. Todd said that Ryan should be fine so he took the other kids and left Ryan in front of the television to watch a NASCAR race. As I was dozing on the bed, I could hear Ryan coming up the stairs. Then the next thing I hear is Todd yelling my name over and over in a panicked tone. I finally came to full conscience when he was right next to the bed hovering over me.

"Thank God!" Todd exclaimed.

"What's the matter? I thought you were going to Target." I questioned.

"We did. Do you know where Ryan is?" He asked. I thought Todd was kidding when he said that they had already been to Target and back again.

"Up here, I guess. I just heard him come up the stairs." I explained.

"Well, he's not, he's on the couch downstairs, and he's dirty." Todd said.

"What?" I sat up and came to clear conscience.

He told me to come downstairs with him. So I got up, put my glasses on, and followed him downstairs. Todd explained that when they had returned home, the garage door was up, the door connecting the garage and the kitchen was open, and there were hotdog buns all over the driveway! At first I was in disbelief, but I saw it with my own eyes. Todd continued to tell me that he was scared at first because he didn't know if I had been killed or the whereabouts of Ryan. But then he heard Ryan squealing. And then he'd noticed that he'd run over the hot dog buns with the truck. So what really happened? Our synopsis of

83

the situation goes something like this: Ryan managed to get over the gate blocking the kitchen, unlocked the door that connects the kitchen to the garage, went into the garage, pushed the button that opens the garage, went to the refrigerator located in the garage, grabbed the first thing he saw, which was a package of hotdog buns, and went outside with them. Now, how he got back inside safely over the gate, is beyond my comprehension. Indeed, it's a miracle that he wasn't lost in the cove, lost in the neighborhood, kidnapped, or hurt. It's even more miraculous that he was back inside sitting on the couch by the time Todd and the others arrived home. And where was I during this whole episode? Apparently I was fast asleep upstairs in bed. I was sleeping so sound, that I didn't hear the garage door, Ryan squealing, nor did I hear Todd come home. Clearly, God's angels are with us day and night and His hedge of protection is wonderful.

## Sisters are a gift from God

One of Ryan's sisters, Jessica, has taken a special interest in him. She was there in the delivery room when Ryan was born. Somehow I believe that bonded them for life. She is in the fifth grade and at the same school as Ryan and their youngest sister, Hannah. Jessica volunteers in his class on Fridays and helps the most with him at home. She even accompanies us on his field trips. She watches out for him when they are outside playing with the neighborhood children. She makes sure no one treats him unfairly or picks on him at school on the playground. During lunchtime Jessica's class comes into the cafeteria after Ryan's class. She often purchases extra drinks or snacks for him out of her own lunch money. Some of the most precious times they have shared are during the night and early mornings. Some days I wake up to find Jessica sleeping on the floor beside Ryan's bed. As I look around I notice that he must've woken her up during the night. Jessica will get up make him a drink, snack, and put in a long video for him. Then she'll cover him up with his blanket when he's finished eating. He'll go back to sleep and she'll fall asleep with him. And the sweetest thing is that I never knew Ryan was awake or what happened. She's played the caregiver and let me sleep.

Ryan's oldest sister, Sarah is a blessing from the Lord as well. When Ryan has a poop emergency, I will clean up Ryan and come back and Sarah has already cleaned up the poopy mess left behind. What other teen does that? She goes with us to his doctor appointments, emergency room trips day or night, and helps me with Ryan out in public. She helps me lift him and move him when he won't move his own body. She takes Ryan swimming and watches him in the swimming pool. She is very protective over Ryan, especially when other kids make fun of him.

Sarah and Jessica both help give Ryan baths and change his diapers when I'm unavailable. They are terrific sisters and we are grateful that the Lord would bless us with them.

Ryan's baby sister, Hannah who is eight, is a whole lot smaller than Ryan and doesn't interact with him as much. The main reason for this is that Ryan pushes her down and sits on her. So she tries and stays away from him as much as possible. But she helps me in her own way with Ryan. She will bring me diapers, wipes, drinks, medicine and anything else I need when caring for Ryan. She even cleans up his room when video tapes and toys get scattered everywhere. So she is a huge help as well in her special way.

So they each contribute their time helping with Ryan in the specific way God enables them.

## Big Brothers are a 'Gift from God' as Well

Literally this is the truth! Matthew actually means 'a gift from God.' When Matt is around he helps significantly with Ryan too. In fact, if I need Ryan anywhere Matt will pick him up and put him over his shoulder and walk with him like a sack of potatoes to wherever I need him. And now that I think about it, if I want to move to another room in the house or visit a neighbor in our cove, Matt will pick me up as well and carry me to where I want to be. He towers over us and is very strong and will just pick us up and take us there. He also helps keep Ryan's room clean, takes out bags full of Ryan's diapers and will even put away Ryan's laundry when reminded to do so. He will take Ryan into another room when I'm trying to have a phone conversation. He himself will leave me alone during a phone call. He won't even be nosy and try and figure out what we're talking about. Now, that's a mega blessing in itself! I wish the girls would take note as well and leave me alone when I'm on the phone. Oh well, I guess I can't have everything!

## Bragging on Dad

The following clips are me bragging about my wonderful husband as a terrific Dad. He is great with the girls but special relationship that he has with Ryan is incredible and God given.

## Between Father and Son

My husband, Todd, is the best Dad I know. He is the neighborhood 'big kid'. He plays with the other children in our cove but corrects them when necessary. He is especially good with Ryan. At first Todd was apprehensive about being Ryan's Dad as he thought Ryan's handicaps were his fault. But after working through the false guilt Todd is fine with Ryan. It also took him years to not be embarrassed of Ryan and even now once in a while he still seems uneasy when we're all out in public together. But overall, Todd is great with him. Ryan loves wrestling with him. Ryan will wobble up to him and just slap him on top of the head. He'll back up like he's casing his father and then jump onto his lap and just giggle. Ryan loves getting showers with him but Todd says Ryan's getting so big they can't both fit in the shower as well as they used to when Ryan was smaller. One morning as I was making our bed, apparently Ryan had slipped and tried to hold himself up. I overheard Todd yell, 'NO, Ryan! *THAT'S* NOT a handle! I laughed. The next word I heard was my name. Todd was calling me to come get him OUT!

Todd will often come home and take Ryan through McDonald's. They drive around and sightsee because Ryan loves driving around town. As long as he has music, Ryan loves car rides. I can just hear Ryan saying, "Ah, this is the life, McDonald's cheeseburgers, fries, and COKE®, loud music, and riding around in the car!"

Todd will often play with Ryan in the pool and play ball with him. Todd will throw the ball to Ryan. Ryan will block it. (Sometimes I wonder if Ryan could spike the ball in volleyball) Ryan picks up the ball and throws it back. They watch NBA basketball together, watch NASCAR races together, and they *definitely* watch Shania Twain videos together. Their father and son bonding times are wonderful. They even take naps together! Truly, 'It's A Wonderful Life.'

## Ryan's Hope

If you live in the Memphis area and there is 'a special needs' someone in your life, whether he/she is family or friend, please come visit us at Ryan's Hope. Ryan's Hope is more than a support group for family and friends of special needs people. It is a place to come for hope, love, acceptance, resources, small group time, inspiring words, and of course food! If you are interested in learning *how to* help those in your community who are caring for differently abled children in their lives, please come check us out! We meet at Christ the Rock Church in Memphis. Please call 901-751-3333 for more information and meeting times. If you are interested in starting your own Ryan's Hope Outreach Ministry please contact us at Ryan's Hope c/o Christ the Rock Church 8800 Winchester Rd. Memphis, TN 38125.

## A.S.K. Bible Studies

If you are interested in learning how to read and study God's Word and learning how to apply it to your life today, contact A.S.K. Bible Studies @ ask@midsouth.rr.com